from SEA TO SHINING SEA

UTAH

By Dennis Brindell Fradin

CONSULTANTS

Michelle J. Schick, Utah State Historical Society, Salt Lake City

Robert L. Hillerich, Ph.D., Consultant, Pinellas County Schools, Florida;
Visiting Professor, University of South Florida

CHILDREN'S PRESS
A Division of Grolier Publishing
Sherman Turnpike
Danbury, Connecticut 06816

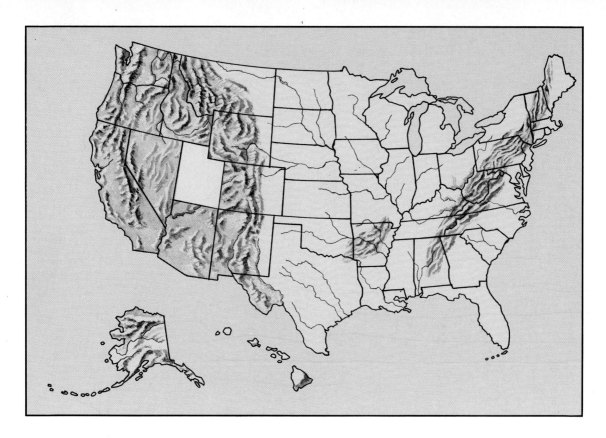

Utah is one of the six Rocky Mountain states. The other Rocky Mountain states are Colorado, Idaho, Montana, Nevada, and Wyoming.

For Arielle Joy Polster from Uncle Dennis with love

For their help, the author thanks Dr. Glen M. Leonard, Director, Museum of Church History and Art, Salt Lake City; and Dr. Floyd A. O'Neil, Director, American West Center, Adjunct Professor of History, University of Utah.

Front cover picture: mesas and cliffs around Soda Springs Basin, Canyonlands National Park; page 1, Bonneville Salt Flats; back cover, Mormon Temple, Brigham City

Project Editor: Joan Downing
Design Director: Karen Kohn
Research Assistant: Judith Bloom Fradin
Typesetting: Graphic Connections, Inc.
Engraving: Liberty Photoengraving

SECOND PRINTING, 1994.

Library of Congress Cataloging-in-Publication Data

Fradin, Dennis B.
  Utah / by Dennis Brindell Fradin.
    p.   cm. — (From sea to shining sea)
  Includes index.
  Summary: An overview of the Beehive State, introducing its history, geography, sites of interest, and famous people.
  ISBN 0-516-03844-3
  1. Utah—Juvenile literature. [1. Utah.] I. Title.
II. Series: Fradin, Dennis B. From sea to shining sea.
F826.3.F69   1993   92-36370
979.2—dc20   CIP
                                   AC

Table of Contents

A father takes his daughter hiking in Capitol Reef National Park.

INTRODUCING THE BEEHIVE STATE

*U*tah is a large state in the western United States. It was named for the Ute Indians. A religious group called the Mormons started settling Utah in 1847. They named their new homeland *Deseret*. That's a Mormon word meaning "honeybee." The Mormons worked like bees to build Utah. Later, Utah was nicknamed the "Beehive State."

The Beehive State is known for its natural wonders. The Great Salt Lake is in Utah. Because this lake is so salty, people can easily float in it. Mountains, canyons, and deserts add to Utah's charm.

Salt Lake City is the state capital. The Mormon church has its world headquarters there. It is also home to the Mormon Tabernacle Choir.

Utah is special in other ways. Where was the golden spike driven in to complete the first cross-country railroad? What state has the highest percentage of people who can read? Where have cars raced at more than 600 miles per hour? Where was Newbery Medal winner Virginia Sorensen born? The answer to these questions is: the Beehive State!

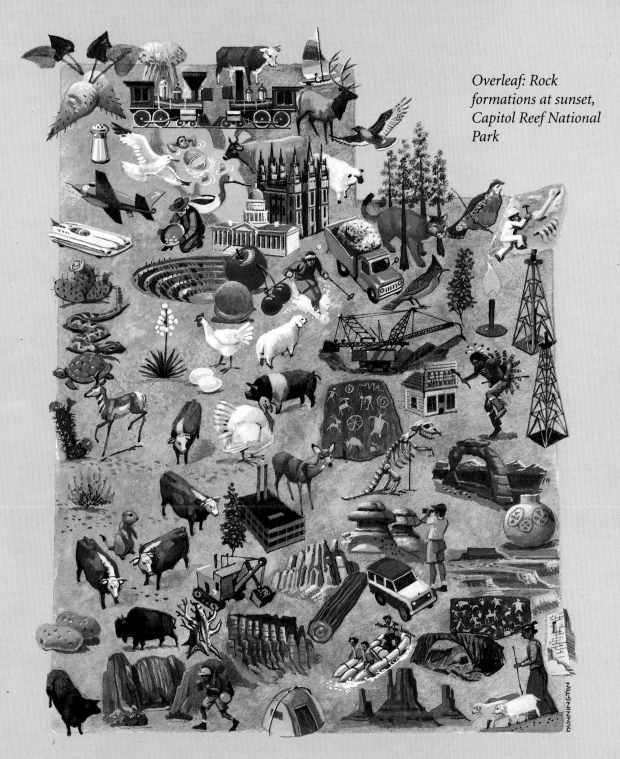

Overleaf: Rock formations at sunset, Capitol Reef National Park

A picture map of Utah

Mountains, Deserts, and the Great Salt Lake

MOUNTAINS, DESERTS, AND THE GREAT SALT LAKE

The Four Corners Monument marks the place where the states of Utah, New Mexico, Arizona, and Colorado come together.

Mount Timpanogos is in the Wasatch Mountains.

Utah covers nearly 85,000 square miles. It is one of four states with straight lines for borders. Wyoming, Colorado, and New Mexico share this feature with Utah. All three border the Beehive State. Wyoming is Utah's neighbor to the northeast. Colorado is to the east. New Mexico touches Utah's southeastern corner. Arizona is to the south. Nevada is to the west. Idaho lies to the north.

The Rocky Mountains run through northeastern Utah. Utah's Uinta and Wasatch ranges are part of the Rockies. Utah's highest point, Kings Peak, is in the Uinta Mountains. Kings Peak is 13,528 feet high. The Colorado Plateau covers most of eastern and southern Utah. It has many canyons and cliffs.

The western third of Utah is desert. The Great Salt Lake Desert is west of the Great Salt Lake. The Escalante and Sevier deserts are in the southwest.

LAKES AND RIVERS

The country's largest lake west of the Mississippi River is in Utah. This is the Great Salt Lake. It cov-

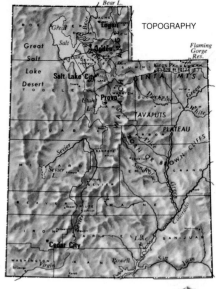

TOPOGRAPHY

ers more than 1,700 square miles. Its water does not drain into streams or rivers. Rivers that flow into the lake deposit salt. Some of its water evaporates and leaves salt behind. That's why the Great Salt Lake is so salty. Salt and magnesium are mined in the lake.

Utah Lake and Bear Lake are the state's biggest freshwater lakes. The Colorado and the Green are Utah's major rivers. Utah's freshwater lakes and rivers provide water for people and crops. Canals carry this water to the state's cities and farms.

CLIMATE

After Nevada, Utah is the driest state. The Great Salt Lake Desert is Utah's driest region. It averages

The Manti-La Sal National Forest (above left) is in the Colorado Plateau. Utah Lake (below) and Bear Lake are the state's two biggest freshwater lakes.

Coral Pink Sand Dunes State Park (left) gets between 8 and 12 inches of rain each year. The Uinta Mountains (right), however, can get more than 50 inches.

less than 5 inches of rain and snow a year. Some parts of the country can get that much rain in a day. Utah's mountains, though, receive about 50 inches of rain and snow each year.

The higher the area in Utah, the cooler the weather. Winter temperatures can get very cold in Utah's mountains. The state's record low temperature was minus 69 degrees Fahrenheit. This happened in northern Utah near Logan on February 1, 1985.

Utah's deserts can get very hot in the summer. The state's record high was 117 degrees Fahrenheit. This occurred at St. George in southwest Utah on July 5, 1985.

PLANTS AND ANIMALS

One-third of the Beehive State is forest. Most of the forestland is in Utah's mountains. Blue spruce is the state tree. Firs, pines, willows, and poplars also grow in Utah.

Wildflowers clothe Utah in bright colors. The sego lily is the state flower. Other Utah wildflowers include yuccas, desert sunrays, and Indian paintbrush. Cactus plants grow in Utah's deserts.

Many wild animals live in Utah. Black bears, buffaloes, mule deer, elks, and pronghorn antelopes are all found in Utah. Porcupines are found in the mountains. Ringtail cats also live in Utah. They look like cats but are in the raccoon family. Wild horses called mustangs run free in the desert valleys. Desert tortoises, rattlesnakes, and lizards called Gila monsters also live in Utah's deserts.

Sea gulls nest around the Great Salt Lake. The sea gull is the state bird. Eagles and hawks fly about the Beehive State.

Slickrock paintbrush is one of the bright wildflowers that thrive in Utah.

Rattlesnakes live in Utah's deserts.

11

From Ancient Times Until Today

FROM ANCIENT TIMES UNTIL TODAY

More than 140 million years ago, dinosaurs lived in Utah. Allosaurus, Utah's state fossil, lived there. So did diplodocus and stegosaurus. Bones from many other dinosaurs have also been found in Utah. They were found at Dinosaur National Monument. That is in northeastern Utah. Dinosaur tracks have been discovered in southern Utah.

About 2 million years ago, the Ice Age began. Sheets of ice covered part of northern Utah. Mammoths and mastodons were in Utah during this cold period. They were relatives of today's modern elephants.

Anasazi cliff dwellings in southern Utah

AMERICAN INDIANS

People first reached Utah at least 12,000 years ago. These first Utahns were ancient Indians. They picked berries and hunted animals. They lived in caves. About 2,000 years ago, the Anasazi lived in southern Utah. By A.D. 500, they were growing corn, beans, and squash. They built rock houses along cliffs and canyons. These early people carved

The people of Utah are called Utahns.

Opposite: Newspaper Rock, with its ancient Indian rock art

13

Petroglyphs (rock carvings) at Dinosaur National Monument

Left: Paiute wickiups
Right: Utes gathered for the Bear Dance

and painted pictures on cliffs. Newspaper Rock in southeast Utah contains many rock carvings. The early people made them over a period of 1,500 years.

Four major American Indian groups lived in Utah by the 1700s. They were the Utes, Paiutes, Shoshones, and Gosiutes. The Utes and Shoshones lived in tents called tepees. The Paiutes and Gosiutes lived in huts called wickiups. They ate pine nuts, sunflower seeds, and roots. Some grew corn and squash. Many hunted buffaloes, deer, and rabbits. Paiutes and Shoshones made cakes of grasshoppers mixed with berries. In the 1800s, the Indians gave these cakes to hungry settlers. The settlers called them "grasshopper fruitcakes."

The Indians had special dances and enjoyed sports. The Utes still perform the Bear Dance each spring. The Shoshones played a kind of football. They used balls made from animal skins.

EUROPEAN EXPLORERS AND AMERICAN MOUNTAIN MEN

Spaniards were the first European explorers in Utah. Juan Maria Rivera explored southeastern Utah in 1765. Two Spanish priests, Fathers Domínguez and Escalante, arrived in 1776. They explored northeastern Utah. Utah was under Spain's rule. Spaniards did not settle in Utah, however.

In 1776, Americans along the Atlantic Ocean formed a new country. They called it the United States. American mountain men entered Utah in the 1820s. By then, Utah was under Mexico's control. The mountain men traveled through the Rocky Mountains trapping beavers and other animals. These men also traded with the Indians for furs. The furs were used to make hats and clothing.

In 1824, mountain man Jim Bridger arrived at the Great Salt Lake. He became the first known non-Indian to see the lake. The mountain-man era

Mountain men such as Jim Bridger (above) trapped beavers and other animals in the Rocky Mountains.

in Utah ended about 1840. By then, the beaver supply had run low.

THE MORMONS SETTLE UTAH

The story of the settling of Utah begins in New York State. There, in 1830, Joseph Smith, Jr., founded the Church of Jesus Christ of Latter-day Saints. It is also called the Mormon church. Members are called Mormons or Latter-day Saints.

Mormons believed that Jesus Christ appeared in America after his death. They also believed that families come together again in heaven after death. Mormon men could practice polygamy. That means they could have more than one wife at a time.

Because of these beliefs, life for the Mormons was hard. Non-Mormons didn't want them in their towns. The Mormons were pushed to Ohio and then to Missouri. In 1839, they founded Nauvoo, Illinois. By the early 1840s, Nauvoo was Illinois's largest city. But non-Mormons still did not understand the Mormons' beliefs. Mormon farms and crops were burned in an effort to drive the Mormons away. On June 27, 1844, a mob murdered Joseph Smith and his brother Hyrum.

Brigham Young then became the Mormon lead-

Joseph Smith, Jr., founder of the Mormon church

westward. In 1846, thousands of Mormons set out on the long westward journey. In July 1847, Young led an advance party of about 170 Mormons into the Great Salt Lake Valley.

"This is the place," Young said, on July 24. Near that place, the Mormons founded Salt Lake City. July 24 became a holiday called "Pioneer Day" in Utah.

The Mormons called their new homeland Deseret, meaning "honeybee." The Mormons worked like honeybees. They plowed fields. They planted crops. They dug canals to bring water to their fields. They laid out streets in Salt Lake City. A

Covered wagons like those used by the Mormon pioneers can be seen at Pioneer Trail State Park.

piece of land was set aside for the Mormon Temple and the Mormon Tabernacle. Utah's first school opened three months after the Mormons arrived. Sixteen-year-old Mary Jane Dilworth was the teacher.

The Mormons planted wheat and corn that first year. There wasn't much of a harvest, though. People survived on sego lily bulbs. That is why the sego lily became the state flower. During the second year, 1848, millions of grasshoppers attacked the crops. Sea gulls from the Great Salt Lake came to the settlers' aid. The gulls ate the grasshoppers. The sea gull was later named Utah's state bird.

UTAH BECOMES A TERRITORY

Mormons kept pouring into Utah. Ogden, Provo, Manti, and Tooele were all settled by 1850. In that year, Utah had a population of more than 11,000. Also in 1850, the University of Deseret was founded in Salt Lake City. It is now the University of Utah. Utah's first newspaper was the *Deseret News*. It was published in Salt Lake City in 1850. It is still published today.

In 1848, Utah's land had become part of the United States. Most people in Deseret wanted to become a United States territory. The United States

The type of grasshopper that attacked the crops was named the Mormon cricket.

The Utah Territory seal featured a beehive with sego lilies on either side. These symbols are now part of the state coat of arms and the flag.

Congress did this in 1850. Brigham Young was named governor. But Congress rejected the Mormon name of Deseret. The name was changed to the Utah Territory.

Early Utahns worked very hard to make their land productive.

INDIAN WARS, THE UTAH WAR, AND THE GOLDEN SPIKE

Brigham Young and others had spread Mormonism in Europe. Thousands of Mormons moved to Utah in the 1850s. They came from the United States and Europe. Some non-Mormons also arrived.

Utah's Indians were angry. The newcomers were taking their lands. The Utes began attacking settlers in 1853. This was the Walker War. It was named for Wakara, a Ute chief. The settlers called him Walker. Brigham Young and Wakara met near Nephi in 1854. The two leaders made peace.

The Utah War (1857-1858) began because of religious tensions between Mormons and non-Mormons. Non-Mormons complained of the same abuses and prejudice at the hands of the Mormons that the Mormons themselves had suffered. As a result, President Buchanan sent troops and a new governor into Utah. Mormons then attacked and killed 120 non-Mormons. This is known as the Mountain Meadows Massacre. Fearing punishment by the federal government, the Mormons agreed to remove Brigham Young as governor. The army left in 1861.

From 1865 to 1868, the Utes once again attacked the settlers. Chief Black Hawk led his people in the Black Hawk War. In the end, the Indians could not defeat the settlers. The Utes were forced onto reservations near the Uinta Mountains.

In 1869, two railroads completed laying track across the country. The two lines met at Promontory, Utah, on May 10, 1869. A golden spike was pounded into the last railroad tie. It connected the railroads. The East Coast and West Coast were then linked by rail.

There was another Chief Black Hawk. He led the Sauk and Fox in Illinois and Wisconsin in the 1830s.

The Union Pacific Railroad worked toward the west. The Central Pacific Railroad worked toward the east.

20

A NEW STATE DEVELOPS

By 1880, more than 143,000 people lived in the Utah Territory. Utah was ready for statehood. Congress said no. Many Mormon men still practiced polygamy. In the 1880s, Congress passed laws to end polygamy. But the Mormons ignored the laws. The government took away the voting rights of about 12,000 Mormons. More than 1,000 Mormons with more than one wife were jailed.

Finally, in 1890, the Mormon church outlawed polygamy. This paved the road to statehood. Utah became the forty-fifth state on January 4, 1896. Its

When two railroads met in Utah in 1869, a golden spike was pounded into the last railroad tie.

Only about one Mormon man in twenty had more than one wife at one time.

21

constitution outlawed any new multiple marriages. Women gained the right to vote.

Until the 1920s, Utah enjoyed a mining and farming boom. The state became a major producer of coal, copper, and silver. New irrigation projects brought water to farms and ranches. Cattle raising and sheep raising grew in importance.

Utah's scenic and historic sites became known throughout the country. Natural Bridges National Monument was founded in 1908. Zion National

Sheep raising (left) and mining (right) were important in Utah in the early 1900s.

Park was set aside in 1909. Dinosaur National Monument was founded in 1915.

In 1917, the United States entered World War I (1914-1918). About 21,000 Utahns served. At home, Utahns also helped win the war. They mined metals and made weapons.

In the early 1920s, many mines closed. Then, in 1929, the Great Depression hit the United States. This was a ten-year period of hard times. More Utah mines closed. Banks went out of business. Droughts and low prices for farm goods hurt Utah's farmers. By 1933, one-third of Utah's workers had lost their jobs. This was one of the highest jobless rates for any state, ever.

United States government projects helped the country through the hard times. Some projects in Utah helped farmers. Some built roads and bridges. Others put up public buildings. The Mormon church also had programs to help its members.

World War II (1939-1945) helped end the Great Depression. The United States entered the war in 1941. About 70,000 Utahns served. More than 100,000 Utahns built military bases and made or tested weapons. Wendover Army Air Base was important to the war. The crew that dropped the atomic bomb on Hiroshima, Japan, trained there.

Before child-labor laws were passed, very young children worked in Utah's mines.

About 760 Utahns died in World War I; about 3,700 died in World War II.

UTAH SINCE WORLD WAR II

The Cold War (1948-1989) began shortly after World War II ended. This was not a shooting war. But the United States and Russia greatly feared each other. Both countries built up their weapon supply. Ogden and Salt Lake City made missiles. By 1962, Utah had the most military workers of any state.

Mining also grew. Uranium was found near Moab in 1952. This metal is used in nuclear weapons and nuclear power plants. Utah became a big uranium producer. A few years later, oil also became a major Utah product.

Meanwhile, other Americans were discovering Utah. Many tourists began coming to the state in the 1960s. People came to see Utah's scenic wonders. They skied down its mountainsides. Hotels and ski resorts were built. By the 1970s, five million tourists were visiting Utah each year.

In the past few years, many big firms have come to Utah. They make products ranging from mountain bikes to computer software. By 1994, Utah had one of the country's lowest jobless rates.

Growth in tourism, industry, and mining has attracted many newcomers. Utah's population was just 688,862 in 1950. But by 1990, it had more

Uranium (above) was found in Utah in 1952.

By the early 1990s, 14 million tourists a year were visiting the Beehive State.

than doubled to 1,860,000 people. Few states matched Utah's growth during those forty years. Growth has brought problems, however.

Recently, Utahns have argued about how to use the land. Three-fourths of Utah is owned by the United States government. These lands include national parks and forests. Some Utahns want these beautiful areas preserved forever. Others want some sections opened to industry and mining. That could mean more money and jobs for Utah's people.

January 4, 1996 is Utah's 100th birthday as a state. Many celebrations are planned throughout the state. Utahns will continue to find ways to have both growth and beauty. And the Beehive State will keep growing for another hundred years and beyond.

Utah's national parks, such as Canyonlands (above), attract many tourists to the state.

Utahns and Their Work

Utahns and Their Work

About 12,000 black people live in Utah.

Hispanics are people of Spanish-speaking background. People of Hispanic origin can be of any race; for example, they may identify themselves as both Hispanic and white.

Opposite: Rafting on the Green River

Despite its recent growth, Utah still trails most states in population. Thirty-four states have more than Utah's 1,727,784 people. Only fifteen have fewer. About four-fifths of Utahns live in or near cities. The rest live on farms or in small towns.

Who Lives in Utah?

Nine of every ten Utahns are white. Hispanics are Utah's largest minority. There are about 86,000 Hispanic people in the state. Utah is home to 35,000 Asian people. Utah is also home to about 25,000 American Indians. About 12,000 black people live in the state.

Seven of every ten Utahns are Mormons. The non-Mormons include some 6,000 Catholics and 38,000 Protestants. Jewish people reached Utah by the 1860s. They were among the area's first non-Mormons. Simon Bamberger, Utah's first non-Mormon state governor (1917-1921) was Jewish.

As a group, Utahns are leaders in some important ways. Mormons highly value education. Nine

Utah families enjoy doing things together, even competing in rollerblade contests.

A "median" age of twenty-six means that half the people are older than twenty-six and half are younger.

of every ten Utahns have at least finished high school. Washington is the only state that can match that record. About 95 of every 100 Utahns can read and write well. This is the nation's highest literacy rate.

Mormons especially value family life. That is why Utah has one of America's lowest divorce rates. It has one of America's highest birthrates. It also is the state with the youngest population. The median age of Utahns is twenty-six.

Mormons are counseled not to smoke or drink. As a result, Utahns tend to live longer than people of most other states. Their cancer rate is half the national average.

THEIR WORK

More than 700,000 Utahns have jobs. Service work and selling goods are the leading types of jobs. About 200,000 Utahns do service work. They work in hotels, ski resorts, hospitals, and law offices. Another 170,000 Utahns sell goods. The items range from hamburgers to new cars.

Government work is important in Utah. The state has many government-run parks and forests.

Many Utahns work in the state's national parks, monuments, and forests. Dinosaur National Monument (below) is a popular tourist attraction.

Raising sheep (left) is an important job in Utah. Hay (right) is the state's leading farm crop.

Teachers, too, are counted among Utah's 150,000 government workers.

About 100,000 Utahns make products. Transportation equipment is the leading kind of product. This includes rocket engines, airplanes, and parts for guided missiles. Packaged foods, such as TV dinners, are the state's second-leading product. Other items made in Utah include scientific and computer equipment.

Utah has 13,000 farms and ranches. Beef cattle and milk are the leading farm products. Utah is one

of the top ten states for raising sheep. It's also near the top for growing cherries, pears, and barley. Apples, peaches, hay, wheat, potatoes, and corn are other important farm crops. The Beehive State also produces 1.5 million pounds of honey per year.

About 10,000 Utahns are miners. Utah's most important minerals are oil, coal, natural gas, and uranium. Utah also has gold, copper, iron, and silver. The world's largest beryllium mine is in Utah. This metal is used in rockets, space probes, and VCRs. Utah is one of the top salt-producing states.

Many Utah workers mine coal (above).

Overleaf: The Moab-La Sal Mountains and the Colorado River

31

A Trip Through
the Beehive State

A Trip Through the Beehive State

This is the Place *monument (above) and a statue of Brigham Young (below) are highlights of Salt Lake City.*

*U*tah offers visitors many different sights. The state has one of the world's most unusual lakes. It also has many scenic rock formations. Utahns and visitors alike enjoy outdoor sports. Some of them are skiing, snowmobiling, swimming, boating, hiking, and rock climbing. The Beehive State also has many interesting cities and historic sites.

North-central Utah

Utah's six largest cities are in north-central Utah. They are Salt Lake City, West Valley City, Provo, Sandy, Orem, and Ogden. They lie close to the Great Salt Lake or nearby Utah Lake.

Salt Lake City is Utah's oldest city. *This Is the Place* monument honors Brigham Young and the Mormons. It shows them arriving in 1847. Salt Lake City has been Utah's capital since 1856. It is also Utah's largest city.

The Mormon Temple is at Temple Square in Salt Lake City. This famous building was completed in 1893. It took forty years of work. The highest of

the temple's six spires reaches 210 feet into the sky. *Utah state capitol*
Only active Mormons can enter the temple. It is
used for baptisms, weddings, and other church rites.
The public is welcome, however, at the Mormon
Tabernacle. It is next to the temple. The Mormon
Tabernacle Choir makes its home there. This world-
famous choir is made up of 325 voices and is
accompanied by an 11,000-pipe organ.

The Beehive House is near Temple Square.
Brigham Young lived there with his large family.
Exactly how large his family was is not known.
Some say that Young had twenty-seven wives and
fifty-six children.

Karl Malone (left) is a star forward on the Utah Jazz.

BYU was named for the famous leader who began the school in 1875.

Utah's state government meets at the state capitol in Salt Lake City. Utah's legislature consists of two bodies. One is Utah's twenty-nine-member Senate. The other is the state's seventy-five-member House of Representatives.

The University of Utah is also in Salt Lake City. Work with artificial hearts has been done there. In 1982, Dr. William De Vries placed an artificial heart in Barney Clark. He was the first person to receive one. Two fine museums are also at the University of Utah. The Utah Museum of Natural History has displays on dinosaurs. The Utah Museum of Fine Arts has artworks from around the world.

Salt Lake City is also home to the Utah Jazz. The Jazz is Salt Lake City's pro basketball team.

West Valley City is a suburb west of Salt Lake City. It is Utah's second-largest city. West Valley City is a new city. It was created in 1980 from several other towns. Rocket motors are made there today.

South of Salt Lake City is Provo. It is the state's third-largest city. Provo is on the shore of Utah Lake. The city was settled by Mormons in 1849. It was named for French-Canadian fur trapper Étienne Provost. Brigham Young University (BYU) is in Provo. It is run by the Mormon church. BYU's

Harris Fine Arts Center has works by Mormon artists. BYU is also known for its great athletes. Football stars Jim McMahon and Steve Young went to college there. Baseball and basketball star Danny Ainge went there, too.

Provo has a sister city to the north. This is Orem, Utah's fifth-biggest city. People often refer to the two cities together as Provo-Orem. In 1991, Provo-Orem was named the best place to live in the United States. Orem is known for making computer software.

Sandy is another suburb south of Salt Lake City. It is Utah's fourth-largest city. Begun in 1893, Sandy may have been named for its sandy soil.

The city of Orem, with Mount Timpanogos and the Wasatch Mountains in the background

Sunset over the Great Salt Lake

During the 1980s, Sandy had two claims to fame. It was the United States city with the youngest population. Sandy also had the highest percentage of married people.

Ogden is north of Salt Lake City. It is Utah's sixth-largest city. Utah's oldest pioneer home is in Ogden. Fur trapper Miles Goodyear built this cabin in 1845. Mormons settled Ogden three years later. Today, Ogden is home to Weber State University.

North of Ogden is Logan. It started as a farming and lumber town. Today, Logan has food-packaging factories and women's-clothing plants. It is also home to Utah State University.

NORTHWEST UTAH

The Great Salt Lake covers much of northwest Utah. The lake is seven times as salty as the ocean. Salt makes water buoyant. This water can hold objects afloat better than fresh water. Swimmers can lie in the lake and float like corks. Boating is also popular on the lake.

There are several islands in the Great Salt Lake. Antelope Island is the largest. The antelope are gone. But a buffalo herd now lives on the island. There are also deer, coyotes, badgers, and bobcats. Peregrine falcons, the fastest-flying birds, soar above

Peregrine falcons like this one (above) soar above Antelope Island (below right), which is the largest island in the Great Salt Lake (below left).

the island. They can reach speeds of 220 miles per hour.

The Bonneville Salt Flats are west of the lake. This is a flat, salty desert. A famous auto raceway is at the salt flats. It is called the Bonneville Salt Flats International Speedway. In 1970, Gary Gabelich drove a car there at 622 miles per hour. This is the official speed record for a rocket-powered car.

NORTHEAST UTAH

Dinosaur Gardens has life-size models of dinosaurs.

This dam on the Green River created Flaming Gorge Lake.

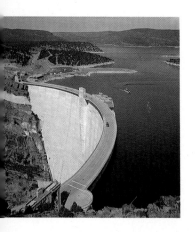

Northeast Utah is nicknamed "Dinosaurland." Thousands of dinosaur bones have been found there. Dinosaur National Monument extends from northeast Utah into Colorado. There, visitors can see many dinosaur bones in an open rock wall. Fourteen life-size models of dinosaurs are at Dinosaur Gardens in nearby Vernal.

Part of northeast Utah is heavily wooded. Wasatch and Ashley national forests are there. These are great places to hike and camp. A trail leads to Kings Peak in Ashley National Forest. At trail's end is Utah's highest point.

A lovely spot in northeast Utah is Flaming Gorge National Recreation Area. Flaming Gorge Lake was made by damming the Green River. Red

rock canyons surround the lake. The Uinta Mountains are south of Flaming Gorge.

South of the mountains is Utah's largest Indian reservation. About 3,000 Utes live on the Uintah and Ouray Reservation. Most of them work for the tribe. Some work in the area's oil fields.

Each summer, a big powwow is held on the reservation. The Utes build "shade houses" at this get-together. These traditional houses are made with cottonwood branches. At the powwow, the Utes perform old dances and play games.

Red sandstone cliffs like this one surround Flaming Gorge Lake.

41

SOUTHEAST UTAH

Moab is southeast Utah's largest city. It has only 4,000 people. In the 1880s, Moab was a farm town. Today, tourism is important there. Moab is between two national parks.

Arches National Park is north of Moab. There are more than 1,500 natural stone arches at the park. The arches were carved over the ages by water and wind. Landscape Arch is one of the world's longest stone arches. It is 306 feet long.

Utah's largest national park is a few miles south of Moab. This is Canyonlands National Park. The Green and Colorado rivers cut canyons through the

Delicate Arch (left) and the Fiery Furnace (right) are two of the natural formations that can be seen in Arches National Park.

rocks. A series of canyons known as the Maze is a highlight of the park.

West of Canyonlands National Park is Capitol Reef National Park. Its rounded sandstone hills look like the Capitol's dome. In the 1890s, outlaw Butch Cassidy hid out there.

South of Canyonlands is Hovenweep National Monument. Indian cliff dwellings there are up to 1,000 years old. Hovenweep is near the Four Corners. There the corners of four states touch. This is the only place in the country where that happens. Visitors can touch Utah, Colorado, Arizona, and New Mexico at the same time.

Left: The Colorado River, in Canyonlands National Park
Right: Hovenweep Castle, an ancient Pueblo Indian ruin at Hovenweep National Monument

Monument Valley

Besides rock arches and cliff dwellings, southeast Utah also has natural bridges. They look much like the arches. However, flowing water in streams created them. Natural Bridges National Monument has three of these bridges. One of the world's largest natural bridges is Rainbow Bridge. It is in far southern Utah near the Colorado River. Rainbow Bridge is 275 feet long. It is as tall as a twenty-nine-story skyscraper.

Monument Valley is between Hovenweep and Rainbow Bridge. There, tall sandstone pillars reach 1,000 feet to the sky. Many movies and television shows have been filmed there.

To the west is Lake Powell. It was formed by the Glen Canyon Dam on the Colorado River. People can boat, fish, and water-ski at the lake.

SOUTHWEST UTAH

Southwest Utah is known as "Color Country." Its canyons and cliffs are red, pink, orange, purple, yellow, and blue. The region's two national parks are famous for their colorful rocks.

Bryce Canyon National Park is southeast of Panguitch. Water, ice, and wind carved the pink cliffs at Bryce Canyon. Bristlecone pines can be seen at this park. Some of these trees are over 4,000 years old. They are the world's oldest living trees.

Zion National Park is west of Bryce Canyon. The Virgin River cut Zion Canyon. This canyon is

Bristlecone pines like these (right) grow in Bryce Canyon (left).

up to 2,400 feet deep and half a mile wide. Ancient sea fossils and Indian cliff drawings have been found at Zion.

Southwest Utah has many towns with buildings but no people. These ghost towns are mostly old mining towns. Grafton is a ghost town south of Zion National Park. The movie *Butch Cassidy and the Sundance Kid* was filmed there in 1969. Frisco is another ghost town. This silver-mining town was a rough place in the late 1800s. Gunmen and gamblers filled the town's twenty-three saloons. In 1885, the Horn Silver Mine collapsed. Most of the people left town.

St. George is a city that is very much alive. It is southwest Utah's largest city. It is in the state's far southwest corner. Its winters are mild. Brigham Young built a winter home there. Today, Young's home is a museum. Utah's first Mormon temple

Sandstone formations in Zion National Park

was completed in St. George in 1877. Each fall, St. George hosts a rodeo.

Cedar City is north of St. George. Each summer, Cedar City hosts the Utah Shakespearean Festival. Plays by William Shakespeare are performed.

North of Cedar City is Beaver. Log cabins and stone houses built by Mormon pioneers attract many visitors.

Fillmore is a good place to finish a trip through Utah. Fillmore was the Utah Territory's capital from 1851 to 1856. The Territorial Statehouse at Fillmore was Utah's capitol. Today, it is a history and art museum.

Left: An abandoned building in the ghost town of Grafton Right: Brigham Young's winter home in St. George

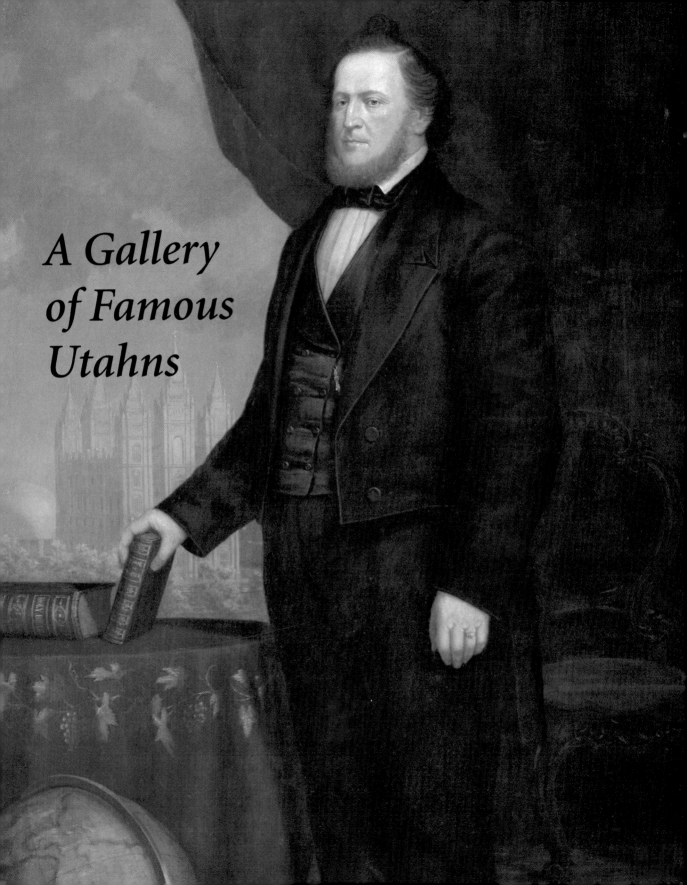

A Gallery
of Famous
Utahns

A Gallery of Famous Utahns

Many Utahns have left their marks on the world. They include religious leaders, lawmakers, singers, and athletes.

Joseph Smith (1805-1844) founded the religion that helped shape Utah. Smith was born in Vermont. In 1830, he founded the Mormon church in Fayette, New York. The church was based on the *Book of Mormon*. These were religious writings. Smith claimed to have obtained them with heavenly help. By 1844, Smith had moved the Mormons to Illinois. Smith decided to run for U.S. president in that year. But a mob in Illinois killed him before the election.

The Book of Mormon *was published in 1830.*

Brigham Young (1801-1877) was also born in Vermont. He joined the Mormon church soon after its creation. Young helped found Nauvoo, Illinois. He became the Mormon leader after Joseph Smith was killed in 1844. Young led the Mormons to Utah in 1847. He brought more than 100,000 people to Utah and other western areas. Brigham City, Utah, was named for him.

Mahonri Young (1877-1957) was born in Salt Lake City. He became a sculptor. Young created Salt

Opposite: Brigham Young

49

Sculptor Mahonri Young designed the Sea Gull monument.

Lake City's *This Is the Place* monument. He also designed the city's *Sea Gull* monument. It honors the bird that saved the crops from the grasshoppers. Mahonri Young also made statues of his famous grandfather, Brigham Young. One can be seen in Salt Lake City. Another is in the U.S. Capitol in Washington, D.C.

Mary Jane Dilworth (1831-1877) was born in Pennsylvania. She came to Salt Lake City in 1847. Dilworth was Utah's first teacher. Her school met in a tent. Dilworth later headed the women's Relief Society for ten years in Huntsville. This Mormon group still helps sick and needy people.

Mary Heathman Smith (1818-1895) was born in England. She became a doctor. In 1862, Dr. Smith moved to Utah. For many years, she cared for people around Ogden. Often, she was paid little or nothing. Smith brought more than 1,500 babies into the world. She still found time to raise her own family of nine.

George Leroy Parker (1866-1912?) was born in Beaver. He became known as **Butch Cassidy.** Cassidy and his "Robber's Roost" gang held up trains and banks in the Rocky Mountain area. Cassidy had a little of Robin Hood in him. He gave some money from his robberies to people who needed help. There are various stories about how and when Cassidy died.

Maude Adams (1872-1953) was born in Salt Lake City. She began her acting career at the age of nine months. Adams played the infant in *The Lost Child*. Later, she became a great actress. Adams was best known for playing the title role in *Peter Pan*.

Reva Beck Bosone (1895-1983) was born in American Fork. She taught high school for a few years. Later, she entered politics. In 1948, Bosone was elected to the U.S. House of Representatives. She was the first Utah woman to do that. As a law-maker, she worked for children's and women's rights.

Le Conte Stewart (1891-1990) was born in Glenwood. He became an artist. Stewart did paintings of simple Utah scenes. He used barns, houses, and farm fields in his works.

Author **Bernard De Voto** (1897-1955) was born in Ogden. De Voto wrote books on the Old West. *Across the Wide Missouri* by De Voto won a

Reva Beck Bosone

Left: Actress Maude Adams in her role as Peter Pan
Right: Butch Cassidy (on the right) and his gang of robbers

Author Virginia Sorensen

Movie star Loretta Young

Pulitzer Prize in 1948. Another author, **Virginia Sorensen**, was born in Provo in 1912. She wrote many adult and children's stories set in Utah. One of her children's books was *Miracles on Maple Hill.* It won the 1957 Newbery Medal.

Philo Farnsworth (1906-1971) was born in Beaver. He became an inventor. While still in high school, Farnsworth worked out the basic idea for television. In 1935, he gave the first demonstration of television.

John Marriott (1900-1985) was born near Ogden. He grew up on a sheep ranch. As a young man, he taught English and ran a bookstore. Later, he entered the hotel business. Marriott founded the Marriott Hotel chain. Today, it has more than 700 hotels.

Simon Bamberger (1846-1926) was born in Germany. He moved to Utah as a young man. There, he earned a fortune in railroading and coal mining. Bamberger was Utah's first non-Mormon governor (1917-1921). He was also its oldest governor. Bamberger took office when he was seventy-one.

Utah has produced some popular entertainers. Movie star **Loretta Young** was born in Salt Lake City in 1914. She won the 1947 Academy Award as best actress in *The Farmer's Daughter*. A brother and sister from Utah became famous singers. **Donny Osmond** was born in Ogden in 1957. **Marie Osmond** was born in 1959. In the 1970s, they hosted the "Donny and Marie" television show. As teenagers, they had many hit record albums.

Gene Fullmer became one of Utah's best athletes. Fullmer was born in West Jordan in 1934. He was the world middleweight boxing champ (1957 and 1959-1962). **Merlin Olsen** was born in Logan in 1940. He was a football star for Utah State University. Later, he played for the Los Angeles Rams. Football quarterback **Steve Young** was born in Salt Lake City in 1961. He is a great-great-great-grandson of Brigham Young. After starring at BYU, Young won fame with the San Francisco 49ers.

Football star Steve Young

Singer Marie Osmond

Home to Virginia Sorensen, Brigham Young, Wakara, Loretta Young, and Philo Farnsworth . . .

Site of the Great Salt Lake, Rainbow Bridge, and ancient Indian ruins . . .

A leading state for raising sheep, growing cherries, and mining gold and silver . . .

The state with the highest percentage of people who can read and write . . .

This is Utah—the Beehive State!

Did You Know?

The world's deepest open-pit copper mine is located near Salt Lake City at Bingham Canyon. It is half a mile deep.

It is thought that the country's first electric traffic light was used in Salt Lake City. The light was installed in 1912. Lester Wire, a Salt Lake City policeman, invented it.

Some movies that have been filmed at Monument Valley include *Stagecoach, Fort Apache,* and *Thelma and Louise.*

In 1896, Martha Hughes Cannon of Utah became the first woman in the United States elected as a state senator. She defeated her own husband to win the post.

The United States Bureau of Land Management has a program by which people eighteen and older can adopt wild horses. To find out about this program, they can write to the U.S. Department of the Interior, Bureau of Land Management, P.O. Box 45155, Salt Lake City, Utah 84145-0155; or call (801) 539-4059.

The honeybee became Utah's state insect in 1983 thanks to the efforts of a class of fifth graders.

Two Miss Americas have hailed from Salt Lake City—Coleen Kay Hutchins in 1952 and Sharlene Wells in 1985.

A liger is an animal that is half lion and half tiger. The first liger born in the United States entered the world at the Hogle Zoo in Salt Lake City on May 6, 1948. She was named Shasta.

Some Hawaiian people who became Mormons moved to Utah. They settled Iosepa, Utah, in 1889. Iosepa is Hawaiian for Joseph, referring to Joseph Smith. Iosepa is now a ghost town.

Brigham Young University won the 1984 National College Football Championship.

On November 4, 1965, Lee Ann Roberts Breedlove became the first woman driver to race more than 300 miles per hour. She did this at the Bonneville Salt Flats.

Timpanogos Cave is in north-central Utah. Hikers discovered it in 1921.

Hogle Zoo in Salt Lake City was home for many years to Princess Alice. This 9,000-pound elephant died in 1953 at the age of seventy-eight.

UTAH INFORMATION

State flag

Sego lilies

Honeybee

Area: 84,899 square miles (the eleventh-biggest state)

Greatest Distance North to South: 345 miles

Greatest Distance East to West: 275 miles

Borders: Wyoming to the northeast; Colorado to the east; New Mexico to the southeast; Arizona to the south; Nevada to the west; Idaho to the north

Highest Point: Kings Peak, 13,528 feet above sea level

Lowest Point: Beaverdam Creek in southwestern Utah, 2,000 feet above sea level

Hottest Recorded Temperature: 117° F. (at St. George, on July 5, 1985)

Coldest Recorded Temperature: -69° F. (at Peter's Sink, near Logan, on February 1, 1985)

Statehood: The forty-fifth state, on January 4, 1896

Origin of Name: Utah was named for the Ute Indians

Capital: Salt Lake City (since 1856)

Previous Capital: Fillmore (1851-1856)

Counties: 29

United States Senators: 2

United States Representatives: 3 (as of 1992)

State Senators: 29

State Representatives: 75

State Song: "Utah, We Love Thee," by Evan Stephens

State Motto: "Industry"

Nickname: "Beehive State"

State Seal: Adopted in 1896

State Flag: Adopted in 1913

State Emblem: Beehive

State Flower: Sego lily

State Bird: Sea gull

State Tree: Blue spruce

State Animal: Rocky Mountain elk

State Fish: Rainbow trout

State Insect: Honeybee

State Fossil: Allosaurus

State Grass: Indian rice grass

State Rock: Coal

State Gem: Topaz

Sea gull

Some Mountain Ranges: Uinta, Wasatch, Grouse Creek, Raft River, Deep Creek, Confusion, Pine Valley, La Sal, Henry

Some Rivers: Colorado, Green, Bear, Weber, Jordan, Sevier, Virgin, San Juan

Some Lakes: Great Salt, Utah, Bear, Sevier

Wildlife: Black bears, mule deer, mountain lions, bobcats, foxes, badgers, skunks, weasels, coyotes, buffaloes, elks, moose, pronghorn antelopes, mustangs, porcupines, ringtail cats, desert tortoises, rattlesnakes, Gila monsters, sea gulls, eagles, falcons, ducks, geese, many other kinds of birds

Indian rice grass

Rocky Mountain elk

Farm Products: Beef cattle, milk, sheep, turkeys, hogs, cherries, pears, barley, eggs, apples, peaches, hay, wheat, potatoes, corn, honey, potted flowers, shrubs

Manufactured Products: Rocket engines, space probes, other transportation equipment, packaged foods, scientific and computer equipment, chemicals, furniture, lumber, clothing, bicycles

Mining Products: Oil, coal, natural gas, uranium, gold, copper, silver, beryllium, salt, gilsonite, molybdenum

Population: 1,727,784, thirty-fifth among the states (1990 U.S. Census Bureau figures)

Major Cities (1990 Census):

Salt Lake City	159,963	Ogden	63,909
West Valley City	86,976	Taylorsville-Bennion	52,351
Provo	86,835	West Jordan	42,892
Sandy	75,058	Layton	41,784
Orem	67,561	Bountiful	36,659

UTAH HISTORY

The University of Utah was founded in 1850

10,000 B.C.—Prehistoric Indians first reach Utah

A.D. 1765—Juan Maria Rivera explores Utah for Spain

1776—Two Spanish priests, Fathers Domínguez and Escalante, explore Utah

1824—Mountain man Jim Bridger becomes the first known non-Indian to see the Great Salt Lake

1844—Joseph Smith, founder of the Mormon church, is murdered in Illinois

1847—The Mormons under Brigham Young arrive in the Great Salt Valley

1848—The United States gains control over Utah and other western lands by winning the Mexican War

1850—The United States Congress creates the Utah Territory; the University of Deseret (now the University of Utah) is founded

1853—Ground is broken for the Mormon Temple in Salt Lake City

1853-54—The Utes and settlers fight the Walker War

1858—United States troops reach Utah; 120 people are killed in the Mountain Meadows Massacre

1865-68—Utes and settlers fight the Black Hawk War

1869—The Golden Spike Ceremony at Promontory marks the completion of railroad tracks across the country

1875—Brigham Young Academy (now Brigham Young University) is founded

1877—Brigham Young dies in Salt Lake City

1890—The Mormon church outlaws multiple marriages

1893—The Mormon Temple is completed in Salt Lake City

1896—Utah becomes the forty-fifth state on January 4

1915—Dinosaur National Monument is founded

1917-18—After the United States enters World War I, about 21,000 Utahns serve

1929-39—During the Great Depression, Utah's mining, farming, and industry suffer

1941-45—After the United States enters World War II, 70,000 Utah men and women serve

1952—Uranium is discovered near Moab

1967—The Central Utah Project is begun to bring water to central Utah

1969—Utah's legislature sets up a program to fight air pollution

1982—The first operation placing an artificial heart in a person is done at the University of Utah Medical Center

1990—University of Utah poet Mark Strand is named poet laureate of the United States

1993—Michael O. Levitt is elected governor

1995—Salt Lake City is chosen as the site of the 2002 Winter Olympic Games

This photo of Manti was taken in 1902, when the population of the state was about 280,000.

MAP KEY

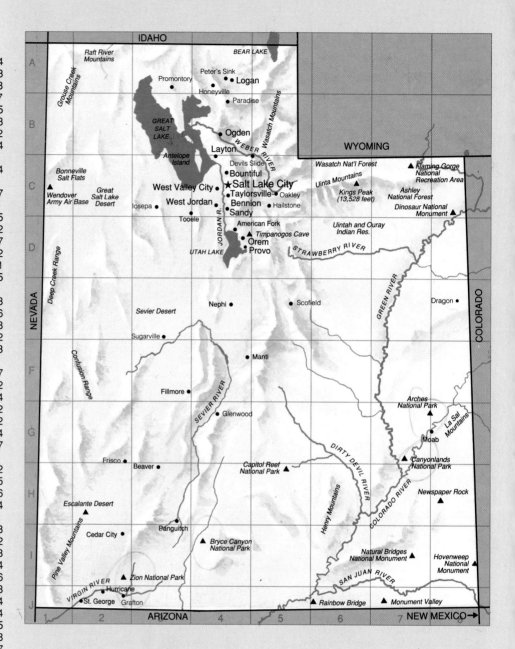

GLOSSARY

ancient: Relating to a time early in history

artificial: Made by people rather than occurring naturally

buoyant: Able to hold objects afloat

canyon: A deep, steep-sided valley

capital: The city that is the seat of government

capitol: The building in which the government meets

climate: The typical weather of a region

desert: An area that receives little rainfall

dinosaur: Generally a huge animal that died out millions of years ago

drought: A period when rainfall is well below normal in an area

explorer: A person who visits and studies unknown lands

fossil: The remains of an animal or a plant that lived long ago

ghost town: A town from which all the people have moved

gorge: A narrow canyon

industry: A kind of business that has many workers to make products

irrigation: A method of bringing water through canals and other artificial means

legislature: The lawmaking branch of government

literacy: The ability to read and write

mammoths and mastodons: Prehistoric animals that were much like the elephants of today

million: A thousand thousand (1,000,000)

missile: A weapon launched over a great distance toward a target

pioneer: A person who is among the first to move into a region

population: The number of people in a place

powwow: A get-together of American Indians

reservation: Land in the United States that is set aside for American Indians

rodeo: A contest in which cowboys and cowgirls ride bucking broncos, rope calves, and wrestle steers

sculptor: An artist who makes statues and other three-dimensional artworks

tepee: A cone-shaped tent made out of animal skins by American Indians of the western plains and mountains

territory: Land that is not yet a state but is under the control of the United States government; its governor is appointed but its people can elect a legislature

tourism: The business of providing services such as food and lodging for travelers

wickiup: A round, grass- or brush-covered hut built by American Indians in dry areas of the west

PICTURE ACKNOWLEDGMENTS

Front cover, © Terry Donnelly/**Tom Stack & Associates**; 1, © Roger Bickel/**New England Stock Photos**; 2, **Tom Dunnington**; 3, © **Virginia R. Grimes**; 5, Tom Dunnington; 6-7, © **Tom Dietrich**; 8 (top), © **SuperStock**; 8 (bottom), © Peter Cole/**New England Stock Photo**; 9 (top left), © E. Drifmeyer/**Photri, Inc.**; 9 (top right), **courtesy of Hammond Incorporated, Maplewood, New Jersey**; 9 (bottom), © **Tom Till**; 10 (left), © David L. Brown/**Tom Stack & Associates**; 10 (right), © **Tom Till**; 11 (top), © David Middleton/**SuperStock**; 11 (bottom), © John Gerlach/**Dembinsky Photo Assoc.**; 12, © **Tom Till**; 13, © Tom Till/**Tony Stone Worldwide/Click Chicago, Ltd.**; 14 (top), © Jeff Foott/**Tom Stack & Associates**; 14 (bottom, both pictures), **Utah State Historical Society**; 15, **North Wind Picture Archives**; 16, **Utah State Historical Society**; 17, © **Tom Till**; 18, **North Wind Picture Archives**; 19, **Utah State Historical Society**; 21, **Utah State Historical Society**; 22 (both pictures), **Utah State Historical Society**; 23, **Utah State Historical Society**; 24, **Utah State Historical Society**; 25, © **SuperStock, Inc.**; 26, © **SuperStock, Inc.**; 27, © Effin Older/**New England Stock Photo**; 28, © Pat Wadecki/**Root Resources**; 29, © Robert Frerck/**Odyssey Productions**; 30 (left), © **SuperStock, Inc.**; 30 (right), © Betty A. Kubis/**R/C Photo Agency**; 31, Betty A. Kubis/**R/C Photo Agency**; 32-33, © **Tom Till**; 34 (top), © **Cameramann International, Ltd.**; 34 (bottom), © **Virginia R. Grimes**; 35, © **Tom Till**; 36, **Wide World Photos, Inc.**; 37, © Peter Cole/**New England Stock Photo**; 38, © **Tom Till**; 39 (top), © Alan G. Nelson/**Dembinsky Photo Assoc.**; 39 (bottom left), Walter Frerck/**Odyssey Productions**; 39 (bottom right), © **Tom Till**; 40 (top), © **Tom Till**; 40 (bottom), © **SuperStock, Inc.**; 41, © **Tom Till**; 42 (left), © Tom Algire Photography/**Tom Stack & Associates**; 42 (right), © Dave Brown/**Tom Stack & Associates**; 43 (left), © J. Blank/**H. Armstrong Roberts**; 43 (right), © **Tom Till**; 44, © **SuperStock, Inc.**; 45 (left), © **Tom Dietrich**; 45 (right), © **Tom Till**; 46, © Buddy Mays/**Travel Stock**; 47 (left), © **SuperStock, Inc.**; 47 (right), © **Tom Till**; 48, © **Salt Lake City**; 50, © **Virginia R. Grimes**; 51 (top), AP/**Wide World Photos**; 51 (bottom left), **Historical Pictures/Stock Montage**; 51 (bottom right), AP/**Wide World Photos, courtesy Nevada Historical Society**; 52 (both pictures), AP/**Wide World Photos**; 53 (top), **Wide World Photos, Inc.**; 53 (bottom), **Associated Press Photo Color**; 54 (bottom), **Utah State Historical Society**; 54-55 (top), © Inga Spence/© **Tom Stack & Associates**; 55 (bottom), UPI/**Bettmann**; 56 (top), **Courtesy Flag Research Center, Winchester, Massachusetts 01890**; 56 (middle), © Stephen Trimble/**Root Resources**; 56 (bottom), © **SuperStock, Inc.**; 57 (top), © Anthony Mercieca/**Root Resources**; 57 (middle), © **Virginia R. Grimes**; 57 (bottom), © Buddy Mays/**Travel Stock**; 58, © **Cameramann International, Ltd.**; 59, **Utah State Historical Society**; 60, **Tom Dunnington**; back cover, © Mauritius-Lindner/**Photri, Inc.**

INDEX

Page numbers in boldface type indicate illustrations.

ABOUT THE AUTHOR

Dennis Brindell Fradin is the author of 150 published children's books. His works for Childrens Press include the Young People's Stories of Our States series, the Disaster! series, and the Thirteen Colonies series. Dennis is married to Judith Bloom Fradin, who taught high-school and college English for many years. She is now Dennis's chief researcher. The Fradins are the parents of two sons, Anthony and Michael, and a daughter, Diana. Dennis graduated from Northwestern University in 1967 with a B.A. in creative writing, and has lived in Evanston, Illinois, since that year.